© Copyright 2016

Written by Sally A Jones and Amanda C Jones
Illustrations by Annalisa Jones

Published by GUINEA PIG EDUCATION

2 Cobs Way,
New Haw,
Addlestone,
Surrey,
KT15 3AF.
www.guineapigeducation.co.uk

NO part of this publication may be reproduced, stored or copied for commercial purposes and profit without the prior written permission of the publishers.

ISBN: 9781910824016

Dear kids,

If you are a fluent reader, you can have fun writing your 'news'. Write down all the things that happen to you everyday in a diary. It will help you develop your writing skills.

Dear parents,

This lively workbook encourages children, of 6-9 years, to write down their own ideas in the form of an informal diary. Writing a diary or 'news' about personal experiences, in your own words, is a wonderful way to get your child writing freely. Your child will also have a record of what he or she has done, which will be fun to read in the future.

A real child's diary has been included, written by a 7 year old, to inspire young writers to record even the smallest details of their daily life. There are also helpful hints on building up sentences to improve writing techniques.

IT IS **FUN** TO WRITE A DIARY

Find yourself a notebook

and a pen or pencil.

Write the date at the
top of the page.

and the day of the week

Jot down all the things that you did today

and how you feel about them.

Write your diary everyday.

Keep it in a safe place.

A the end of the month read your diary.
It will be very interesting.

Ellie Mae wrote a diary.

Saturday 3rd October

On Saturday my big brother went to Scout camp. The moon was shining brightly and we had to walk across a field in the dark to take him there. It was very muddy.

How did Ellie Mae feel?

I felt all spooky in the dark. There were big shadows and I heard an owl hooting in the trees. I felt a bit scared.

The mud was all squelchy. I got mud all over my new trainers. Yuk!

Your turn to write in sentences

- Have you been to a scary place?
- Where did you go?
- Who did you go with?
- How did it feel?

....
....
....
....
....
....
....
....
....
....

Saturday 10th October

When my big brother came home from camp, we went for a walk by the river and we fed the swans and the baby cygnets.

How did Ellie Mae feel?

The baby swan, which is called a cygnet is so cute and fluffy. I wanted to stroke it, but the mother swan wouldn't let me. I felt all shivery because it was so cold.

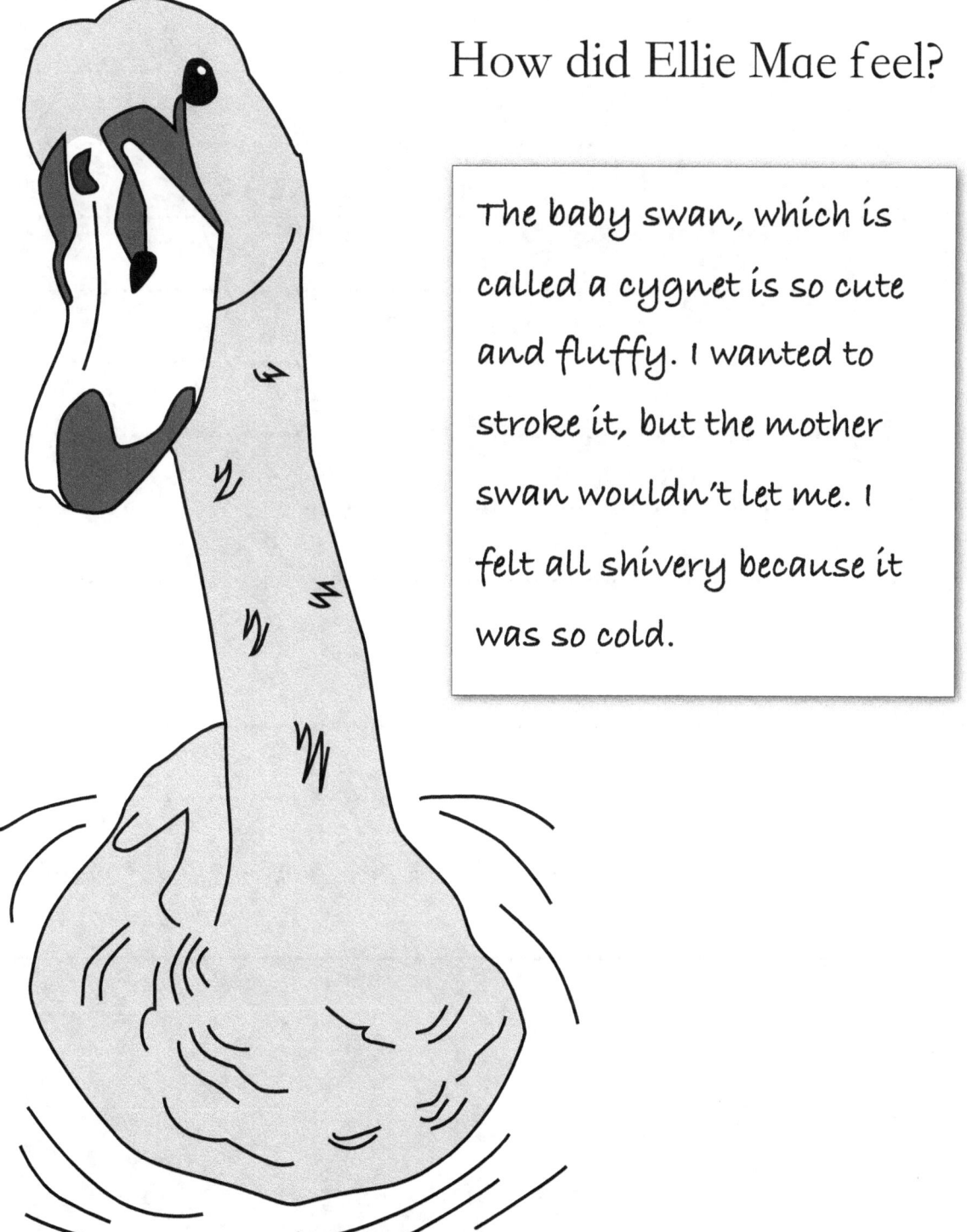

Your turn to write in sentences

- Have you walked by the river?
- What was it like when you walked by the river?

....

....

....

....

....

....

....

....

....

....

....

Monday 12th October

On Monday, I went to school. When I came home from school I baked some cookies. I cut them out in fancy shapes and put icing on them and then covered them in little sugar bits.

Then I got ready for Brownies. I had to make a flower decoration for the table and take my biscuits.

At Brownies we gave the parents the things we had made. My daddy came a bit too late to get some because all mine had gone. Daddy had one of Claire's cheese straws.

How did Ellie Mae feel?

It was fun making the cookies. The cookies tasted really yummy but I was cross with my dad because he was late and he didn't try one of my cookies.

Your turn to write in sentences

- Write about the time you made some cookies.
- What were they like?
- Why did you make them?

....
....
....
....
....
....
....
....
....
....
....

Wednesday 14th October

When I came home from school today, I tried on the outfit I am going to wear for school tomorrow, because it is book week. We have to dress up as a character from a book. I felt excited.

Thursday 15th October

Today we had to dress up as a character from a book. I went as Cruella De Vil from the Hundred And One Dalmatians. In the afternoon we had a fancy dress competition. A girl in my year dressed up as Heidi and won.

I thought it was unfair because my costume was much better.

In the evening, Mummy and Daddy and Olivia came to the Parents Evening at school. They watched me do country dancing with Mrs Cooper. They went round all the classrooms and looked at all the work.

I felt happy because they were pleased with me.

Your turn to write in sentences

- Write about Book Week.
- What costume did you wear?
- Who won the fancy dress competition?
- How did you feel?

....
....
....
....
....
....
....
....
....
....
....

- Write about Parents Evening at your school.

....

....

....

....

....

....

....

....

....

....

....

Friday 16th October

On Friday I had an inset day. Our friends Jackie and Jordan came round. They had lunch with us and then we went to the playground by the riverbank.

After that, we saw the cute baby swan. He has some white feathers now and I think he is really sweet.

Then one of the big swans chased us with his wings fully out. I ran back to the fence because I got really scared, but my friends were laughing at me.

It was nearly dark and it was getting colder every minute. As we walked back along the bank, the headlamps shone into our faces. The lights were so bright that they gave me a headache but when I got home I felt better and I watched some TV.

Your turn to write in sentences

- Write about the time you had some friends come round.
- Did you enjoy it?

....
....
....
....
....
....
....
....
....
....
....
....

- When you go for a walk, where do you go?
- What do you see?
- Which playground do you go to?
- How do you feel?

....
....
....
....
....
....
....
....
....
....
....

Monday 19th October

On Monday I went to Brownies. I had to take a notebook, envelope and a pencil to write a letter, but I forgot it.

I had to borrow a notebook from our leader, but I still got my Hostess badge. Before I went to bed, I showed Mummy my badge.

I felt quite angry with myself for forgetting things but I felt proud to show Mum my badge. My teacher is kind for helping me.

Your turn to write in sentences

- Write about a badge or award you have gained?
- What was it?
- What did you have to do to get it?
- How did you feel?

....

....

....

....

....

....

....

....

....

....

....

....

- Have you ever forgotten something you were meant to take?
- What was it?
- How did you feel?

....
....
....
....
....
....
....
....
....
....
....
....

Wednesday 21st October

On Wednesday I went to school. We did our spelling test and then maths. I got all my spellings right. Cool!

In the afternoon we did art. We painted a picture of somewhere we had been to. My picture was of Sandy Beach. I thought - I wish I were there now.

In the afternoon we also did games. The girls in 3C did games with Mr Wilson and the rest did it with Miss Frost. I got told off for not having my PE kit. When I got home, mum asked me why I was in such a bad mood.

Your turn to write in sentences

- Did you get all your spellings right?
- Do you like painting pictures?
- Do you like P.E.?

....

....

....

....

....

....

....

....

....

....

....

Monday 26th October

HORAY! IT IS HALF TERM!

We went to pick up my friends Claire and Hannah. When we came home we played on the play station.

In the afternoon we drove to the Windsor Great Park. We had to take two cars, because my brother also had his friend round.

When we got there we played football. Then we walked up to the Copper Horse and climbed on the rocks. We played Forty, forty and got really out of breath. Hannah pushed me and I fell flat on my face. I wasn't cross because she didn't mean to do it.

Then we started walking back to the cars. My friends went in the blue car. We watched a film. After that we had tea. We had a yummy dinner of pizza and chips. Then my friends went home.

Thursday 29th October

Yippee! Today, we started our caravan holiday. How exciting! We have come to a campsite in the New Forest with our caravan. When we arrived, daddy parked the caravan and we drove down to the sea. It was raining hard so we got soaked on our walk. The water was dripping down my neck and it felt horrible.

Friday 30th October

On Friday we went to the sea and played on the beach. Then we went to the yummy sweet shop on the pier, which sells big sticky lollipops, which I love. Later we went to Pizza Hut and tried a new pizza from the menu, which was delicious.

Saturday 31st October

On Saturday my brother got on everyone's nerves and got told off. First, he was messing around and fell off the slide in the playground. Then he sneaked away with some older children without asking mum and went to play table tennis but we had to search for him when it was time to go out. I thought he was rather rude.

Later we had a picnic in the car, because it was raining again. We had ham rolls and crisps. I had ready salted flavour, because they are my favourite. Then we walked down to the beach. The sweetie shop was closed so instead we played on the beach.

It was very stormy. I liked the waves because they were crashing onto the beach and leaving lots of white foam. I enjoyed finding interesting shells that had been washed up.

Before we went back to the caravan, we had a ride on the carousel. It went really fast and I was clinging onto my horse.

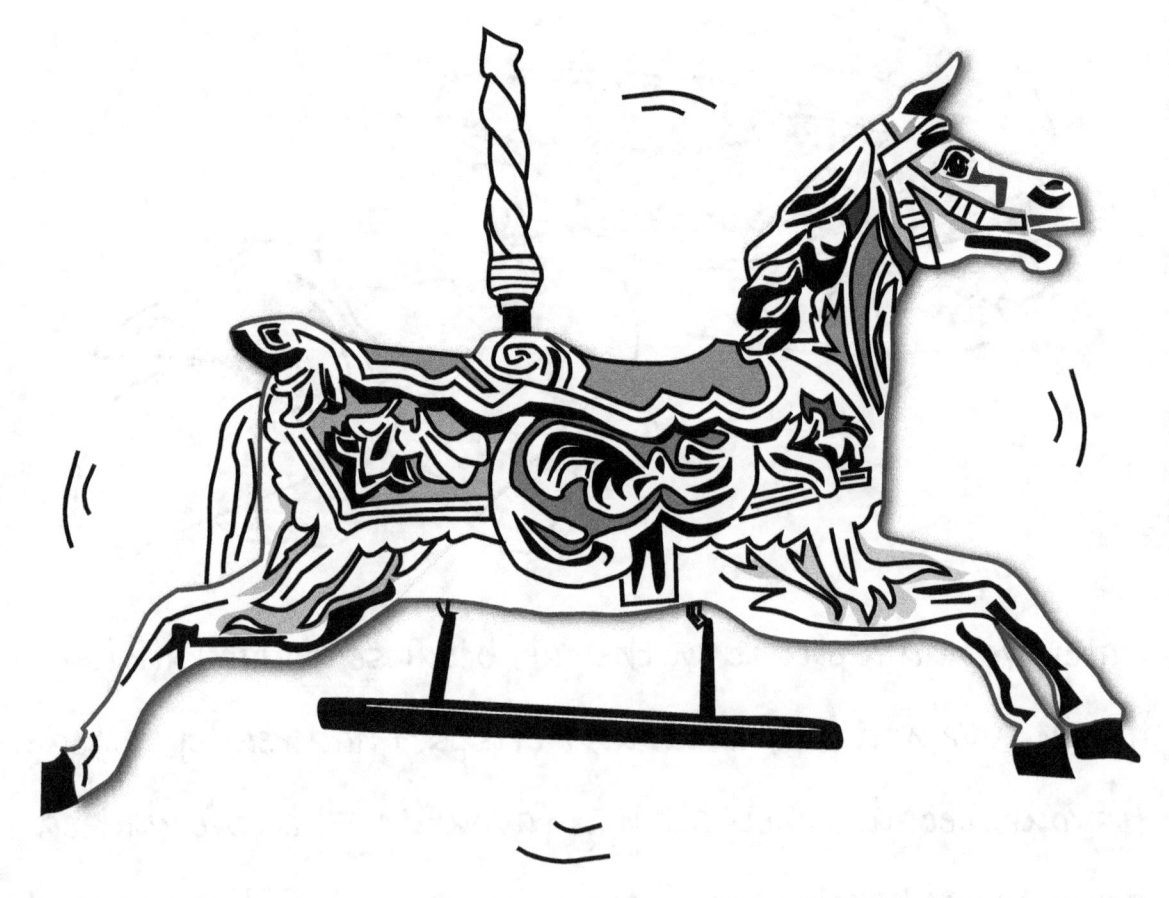

Your turn to write in sentences

- What do you do in half term or on a holiday?
- Write down all those interesting things you did.
- How did you feel?

....

....

....

....

....

....

....

....

....

....

....

....

- Do you have friends round?
- What do you do when your friends come round?

....
....
....
....
....
....
....
....
....
....
....
....
....
....
....

- Is your brother or sister ever naughty?
- What did they do?
- What did you do?
- How did you feel?

....

....

....

....

....

....

....

....

....

....

....

....

....

Tuesday 3rd November

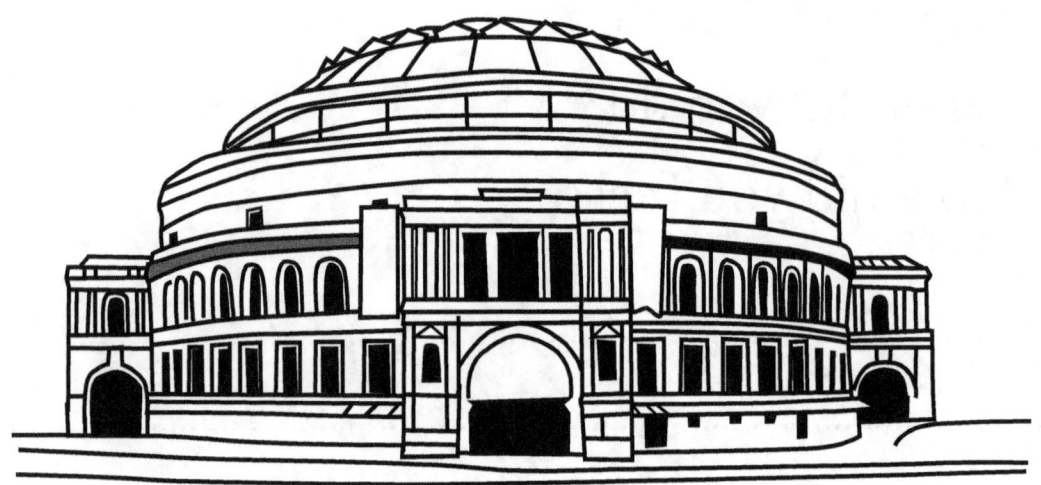

It was Tuesday and I was going to the Royal Albert Hall in London to see my brother in a choir.

When I came home from school I had to have a quick tea and then I had to get changed into my dress. I read my school reading book in the car.

When we got there we had a panic because we could not find our seats and the performance was starting. I just managed to spot my brother, even though he was surrounded by people. I loved the music and seeing the harp and the French horn in the orchestra. I think I would like to learn an instrument. In the interval I had some hot chocolate with cream and marshmallows. It was delicious.

- Have you ever been to a big concert, play or show in a theatre?
- Was it in London or another city?
- What did you see? Was there an orchestra? Did you see instruments? Did you see dancing? Did you see actors?

....
....
....
....
....
....
....
....
....
....
....
....
....

Thursday 5th November

Today it was bonfire night. My brother and I made a guy and put an old shirt, tie and jacket on him. Then we walked the guy to the church. We watched a big firework display, with lots of fireworks. I liked the Catherine Wheel best because it hissed and spluttered and whirled round and round. I also liked the fountains because they had lots of brilliant colours, but the rockets screeched and banged and I found them too noisy.

After the fireworks, they lit the big, roaring bonfire and we put our guy on it. There was lots of food to nibble, like sausages and baked potatoes.

- Have you ever been to a firework display?
- Which one?
- What did you do there?
- How did you feel about it?

....
....
....
....
....
....
....
....
....
....
....

FACT:

Guy Fawkes tried to blow up the Houses Of Parliament in 1605. He was caught, but we remember him on bonfire night by having fireworks and lighting bonfires. It is traditional to make a man out of newspaper, dress him up like Guy Fawkes and burn him on the fire.

Here are some more extracts from Ellie Mae's diary. Imagine what it is like to be her. Add more detail and make them more interesting. Write about Ellie's thoughts and feelings.

> On Monday I went to Brownies and we made a poster about the 20p fair. It was to raise money for charity. We stuck the poster in the window.

Describe a fair you have been to. What did you buy?

> On Tuesday I did not play the right notes in Mrs Urwin's recorder lesson. She wrote a letter to my mum. My mum said I must practise at home.

Have you ever been told off by your teacher? What did you do?

> On Wednesday I went to the Natural History Museum. I bought a ruler and rubber.

Write about a school trip. What did you do there?

On Thursday we bought some plants for our garden Mum did the garden. She took the summer bedding plants out and put in some wallflowers and some pansies.

Have you ever planted some plants in the garden?

On Friday our washing machine broke down so we were in big trouble. I could not go dancing because I had a bad cold.

Write about a day when something in your house broke down.

On Saturday the washing machine was still broken down, so our neighbour did our washing in her machine. Mum was grateful.

Has anyone helped you? What did it feel like?

> On Tuesday we had recorder class. Mrs Urwin said I did not have to go into the beginners class because I played my recorder well.

What does it feel like when you practise something?

> On Sunday we fed the swans again.

What do you do over and over again?

> On Thursday I went dancing. My mum and baby sister went to Notcutts to look at Christmas things and then they picked me up. My big sister went to guides.

How do you prepare for a big festival?

> On Saturday we went to Kingston and bought some Christmas presents for my aunties, uncles and cousins. When we got home my big sister wrapped them up.

What presents have you bought for people?

On Monday it was the 20p fair at Brownies. I got there late. I won the owl because I guessed the owl's birthday correctly. I bought a teddy for my baby sister.

Write about a time when you won something.

On Wednesday we went to the garden centre and filled a bag up with tulip bulbs for the front garden. We also bought four hyacinth bulbs.

On Sunday mum had a bad cold and had to have some of my lemon medicine.

What did you feel like when you had a cold?

On Thursday the washing machine was repaired and mummy did lots of washing. At Brownies we played games. Before I went to bed, I practised my recorder.

On Tuesday, after school, we saw Father Christmas in the department store and told him what we wanted for Christmas. Then we went to the café and bought a hot chocolate.

Have you been to see Father Christmas in a shop? What did you ask him for?

On Wednesday at school I did an audition for the Wizard Of Oz play. After school, we bought a new vacuum cleaner.

Have you been in a school play?

On Thursday, we went late night shopping after school and we bought some advent calendars. I was exhausted when I came home.

Write about a day when you felt tired.

On Friday after school, we went to see my Mum's friend's new baby, called Jonathan.

Ellie Mae uses **three** sorts of sentences.

These are <u>SIMPLE</u> sentences. They have a subject (I) and some action (went shopping). Each sentence has a capital letter and a full stop.

- I went shopping.

- I baked some biscuits.

- Daddy had one of Claire's cheese straws.

- We did our spelling test.

- I read a book.

As children's writing starts to flow more freely, they will use COMPOUND sentences. This is joining two simple sentences using 'and' or 'but'. Remember all sentences have a capital letter and a full stop.

- It was raining very hard and we had to have lunch in the car.

- I went dancing and then I went to the shops.

- It was getting dark and I had tea.

- I forgot my notebook so I had to borrow one.

- I cut them out in fancy shapes and I put icing on them.

- I could not find the cygnet but I fed some other swans.

Finally, as a child progresses up the levels, he or she will start to use complex sentences. These will contain connectives (while, although) and clauses and subordinate clauses.

- My big sister stayed at her friend's house, while we went to the shops.

- I stayed after school because I was in the school choir.

- While we were playing (*subordinate clause*), mummy and daddy did the washing up (*main clause*).

- The swan trod on mum's foot, as she fed him bread.

- After we had finished breakfast, we went on the playground.

- Coming home from school, I got wet in the rain.

- When Daddy came home, we went to the supermarket.

Ellie Maie was 7 years and 5 months when she wrote this diary. She is progressing up the levels, Key Stage 1.

As we have seen, she is using three different sorts of sentence – simple, compound and complex. She uses connectives or joining words like – while, after and because.

She is using full stops and capital letters correctly, but is not using more advanced punctuation, like commas. She says, 'we have sausage and tomatoes and potatoes', rather than using commas.

To make her writing more interesting, she needs to use more detail and to vary her sentences more. She also needs to use better vocabulary, in particular to use more adjectives (amazing fireworks, exciting trip, big trouble, hot chocolate, pretty jumper.)

We bought my baby sister a dress. ✗

We bought my baby sister an incredibly frilly, flouncy, spotty dress, trimmed with ribbon. ✓

www.ingramcontent.com/pod-product-compliance
Lightning Source LLC
Chambersburg PA
CBHW050716090526
44587CB00019B/3402